EME GLORIOUS MESS

That You Are

Unleash Your Inner Goddess

BY
ROSA BERIGUETE

Copyright © 2019 Rosa Beriguete

All right reserved. No portion of this book may be reproduced, stored in a retrieval system, or transmitted in any form or by any means – electronic, mechanical, recording or otherwise (except for brief quotation in printed reviews) without the prior written permission of the author.

The methods describe within this book are the author's personal thoughts, driven by personal experiences and education on the topics discussed. You may discover there are other methods and materials to accomplish the same results.

Published by Rosa Beriguete/Women Empowerment Consulting

www.women-empowermentconsulting.com

Printed in the United States of America

ISBN: 978-1-796-37947-1

Author images by Stephanie C. Olsen Photography

Table of Contents

Foreword 1

Introduction 5

Chapter One: What Holds Women Back? 10

Chapter Two: Cultivating Self-Love And Self-Worth ... 15

Chapter Three: How To Practice Self-Care 22

    Emotionally: 23

    Physically 24

    Professionally: 25

    Mindful Ways Of Shifting Into A Positive Mindset 26

Chapter Four: Define Your Purpose 31

Chapter Five: Vision Boards 34

    How To Use A Vision Board For Goal-Setting 36

    How To Create Inspiring Vision Boards 37

Chapter Six: Rituals For Self-Empowerment 41

Conclusion 44

Foreword

Rosa is a woman dear to my heart. I've seen Rosa from a distance for years, as she would attend various events that I'd organized for my business. Even though she was in the crowd, her support was something that always made her stand out, resonated with me and made me remember her. However, it wasn't until I read her book (pre foreword), that I truly appreciated not just the words ….. but the amazing woman behind the words.

Having six sisters and being the youngest, I've seen most of it all through many female perspectives and survived. I've seen firsthand how strong women are, even with little to no support. This is one of the reasons I'm so passionate about leading, working with, and supporting women.

Trust me when I say, we as women have more in common then we think we do … and hindsight is 20/20. So now I spend my life teaching others and serving others - in various capacities; as a life and business strategist and coach. This in-turn gives me a level of joy that is unexplainable. I am only able to do this, when I am full. So, I have learned to serve others from a full cup and then to replenish.

Self-care is a big thing to me. Eating healthy and fitness are huge to me. Starting the day with meditation and gratefulness changed my world. These things have equipped me to take on what the world brings and are exactly what Rosa, so eloquently, talks about in this book.

We must be aware of and quick to eliminate our negative mental chatter. We must replace and reinforce pure thoughts with positive affirmations! It's extremely important and life changing. Everyday we are presented with a myriad of decisions which could change our lives.

Take the walls down ... it is through that we break down our own barriers and embrace who we are. Keep in mind that it is never too late to want more in your life and change the trajectory of your travels. Start everyday from a mindset of abundance and positive anticipation! You can start small, but believe big. You don't need permission from anyone ... just yourself.

I agreed to write the foreword because I believe in Rosa and her message. She continues to walk the walk, knows what glory is to her, and takes others along with her in these pages. I applaud Rosa for speaking her truth and doing so in a way that resonates with other women. We all have our truths, some we read out loud and some we whisper, as our faith gets stronger. . At the end of the day, we can't keep this stuff bottled up, as it will seep through in all aspects of our life, relationships and self-care.

Getting serious about life is an intentional mindset, that is reinforced by action. Everyday ask yourself, what do you want in life ... and work towards being mindful about who, what and where we spend our time. By the time you finish reading this book, you will be well on your way. Work towards starting everyday with your why, morning devotion and knowing that there is always something to be grateful about.

If you start to implement Rosa's principles of self-care into your life, you are bound to see a dramatic increase in all areas of your life, including how you interact with others and how you see yourself and your life.

Anna M. Foster, CEO
A Maven's World
Connecting People. Empowering Life.
Boston (2019)

YOU ARE POWERFUL, AND WORTHY!

Rosa Beriguete
Empowerment & Spiritual Coach
Reiki Practitioner

Introduction

I dedicate this book to all my "WONDER WOMEN", the full-time mothers, housewives, professionals, entrepreneurs, daughters, friends, my beautiful clients and social media followers who have made me proud to see that in 2018 women have accomplished so much.

Many of us have trouble embracing things we perceive to be imperfection. We are often faced with doubts, setbacks, and failure. While most of us do this anonymously, others have hit roadblocks quite famously. Orville and Wilbur Wright watched a lot of plane crashes before they took off. Twenty-seven publishers turned down Dr. Seuss's first book. J.K. Rowling was a broke single mom when she created Harry Potter.

The key to moving beyond our limiting beliefs and setbacks is resilience. If we didn't go through obstacles in life, we might not be able to discover who we truly are. Self-ownership, truth, and individuality allow us to listen to our inner voice and give us the freedom we need to choose our own path, to start living our life on purpose.

The relationship we have with ourselves can make the difference in the relationships we have with others and even determine how far we can go in life. When we consistently work on becoming better versions of ourselves instead of living our life seeking the approval of others, we open our world to myriads of possibilities. Without fully understanding ourselves, it will be difficult for us to be that person that we seek to become.

Often, we are so hard on ourselves, we forget to love ourselves and what makes us the person that we are. We must stop wanting to appear a certain way to people if we want to emerge from the shadows. After all, we have every right to do as we please. We deserve happiness, irrespective of our shortcomings. Little or big, single parent or divorcee, heartbroken or hopelessly in love, we deserve the very best things in life.

Embracing the glorious mess that we are allows us to be at peace within ourselves, regardless of others' opinion of us. It doesn't make us any less worthy or valuable of a person if someone didn't like us or if we weren't "perfect." By trying to fit ourselves into others' perceptions, we deny the world of all our gifts and who we truly are.

No matter what you're going through — whether it's a break-up, confidence issues, or just general life challenges — this book will help you feel like you're not alone and offer sage advice to help you through.

You were born with an amazing and immeasurable power. This power has made you what - and how - you are now. You may be unconscious of it, but with this power you have created your present reality. Yes, everything that you are, have experienced and are experiencing is a result of this power.

How it all started? At some point, I was homeless and ended up in a shelter with a toddler. I was abused and battered by someone I thought cared about me. However, I wasn't about to let the disappointment of my past keep me down for long. I learned to love myself, and worked on me daily. Today, I am a mom of two wonderful kids (Alexandria & Jonathan), Glam-Ma of twins, a successful professional, a home and business owner, and a Wonder Woman. What I've learned, and my experience is that the places where we have the biggest challenges in our life become the places where we have the most to give if we do the inner work. Embracing the glorious mess that I am gives me such a deep capacity for self-love and self-compassion.

Consequently, this book has been written to help you stop caring so much about what everyone else thinks of you and start becoming your beautiful authentic self. It is only when you work on yourself that you can indeed offer the world the most. You could have your world rocked and still pick yourself up, get back to fighting for you and what you believe in. This book is a great starting point towards your journey of feminine self-discovery.

CHAPTER ONE

What holds women back?

There are, of course, numerous reasons why women are still underrepresented in executive positions. Among them are conflicting attitudes about how women should balance their home and work lives. Just look at the tough spot in which Yahoo's chief executive Marissa Mayer found herself when she took a two-week maternity leave (which some deemed too short).

While many criticize Mayer for setting unrealistic expectations for women in the workplace, I wonder, if she was also under pressure to prove she is well capable of running the company, regardless of what the world may believe.

For others, the stereotype that women are inherently less ambitious than men and lack the confidence needed to steer the ship, holds true. While the first reason is true, I disagree on the second. Some women choose to upend their careers because we are kinder and less selfish. But to say that we fail to advance beyond certain stages in our career because we are less ambitious than men is cray-cray. That said, some women are held back by the following reasons:

- Unhelpful stereotypes. Sometimes, we are mentally restricted by the expectations of society. Some careers/courses are more typically male than women. For instance, the fact that most people consider mathematics/engineering as more male-oriented courses than female make some of us opt out of studying these courses at college.
- Unconscious bias. Unconscious bias is one of the reasons that keep women from attaining leadership roles in community or workplace, as people tend to think, "Oh, she's a little too nice for a tough job." Unfortunately, for us, it seems there is just no way around the situation. Damned if we conform to gender stereotypes, damned if we don't. Act assertive, and people will regard you as being bossy or b*tchy. Act less confident, and you would be considered weak and

lacking leadership skills. Besides keeping women out of senior roles, unconscious bias causes women to be discriminated against during recruitment.

- Personal fears and insecurities. Sometimes, we mentally beat ourselves up, before we even start on anything. This can be a product of our past negative experiences or failures, doubts in our abilities, or low self-esteem. Lack of feelings of confidence and security means we reject ourselves even before others get the chance to turn us down. If we must change things, then it is essential to seek ways to psyche ourselves up, believing that nothing is impossible for us to achieve. No job is too tough for us to handle nor is any height too tall for us to attain.

- Traditional gender roles and social pressure. Whether as mothers, sisters, daughters, wives, or in-laws, social pressure and traditional gender roles tend to hold us back from reaching our full potential. American Society expects that for women, family must come first before career. As a result, we are faced with the dilemma of choosing between spending more time at work or with family. When faced with this choice,

most women tend to lean toward family, making it a lot harder for us to pursue leadership roles.
- Perfectionism. Sometimes, women lack self-confidence no matter how much we have accomplished. Self-doubt impacts negatively on a woman's professional aspirations. Our lack of self-assurance, for instance, means often times, we are likely to hold ourselves back from asking for a raise at the workplace, applying for a new job, or even answering a question, until we are sure we can predict the outcome. Sometimes, we overthink or over analyze situations. We blame ourselves when a professional endeavor goes wrong but are quick to credit circumstance when something goes according to our plan. By discrediting ourselves, we are only confining ourselves to the sticky floor that won't let go of us until we try to free ourselves.

Despite all these reasons, the single biggest factor that holds us back is ourselves. The lack of belief in our own value, worth & ability tempers female ambition & holds women back. Circumstances are only limiting when we allow them. Determination is a powerful force that can shape our attitudes and major life decisions if we decide to put ourselves first for once. Before you give up that dream of yours, before you quit trying, before you surrender all the wonderful plans you have made, ask yourself these questions: "How long will I have to depend on someone who could disappoint me at any moment?", "What if they leave me now?", "Am I good enough for this job?", "Do I have the skills to run my business?". An empowered and confident woman fears nothing and will give anything to attain what she deserves.

CHAPTER TWO

Cultivating Self-Love and Self-Worth

As women, we sometimes have a hard time loving ourselves. This is often because we depend on others to build us up and develop our self-worth so much that we forget to rely on our own beliefs and judgments. In a world where judgments, criticisms, and comparisons are rife, we often get told we are not good enough. Unfortunately, we eventually believe others' narrative. As a result, we become trapped in the negativity bias, focusing more on our weaknesses than our strengths because we have been wired to think so. These undermine our efforts to hold ourselves with the highest regards, culminating in low self-esteem.

I have struggled with a lack of self-love for years. I've experienced feelings of guilt and shame more times than I can count and have regularly sought the approval of others. My experience as a teen mother and someone who was deserted by a loved one when I most needed to be love shaped my feelings about myself. It completely changed my view of life and how I feel about myself. My self-esteem hit rock bottom as I struggled through life for most of my teenage years and never felt worthy enough for intimate relationships.

My experience caused me to build a wall so tall around myself that no one else could tear it down. In my mind, I felt stupid, unlovable and unworthy. These underlined most of the emotional challenges I faced. However, with time, I realized I owe it all to myself to make me happy. I knew then that self-love is crucial if I were to become a fully-actualized individual. This caused me to accept me as I am with all my flaws and weaknesses. Today, I can feel the difference.

I have realized from my experience that we cannot function at an optimal level or reach our full potential for success and happiness unless we cultivate self-love. Low self-esteem undermines our joy with several self-sabotaging behaviors like insecurity, neediness, perfectionism, people-pleasing, complicated and chaotic relationships, and underachievement. Others include passive-aggressiveness, poor social skills, hypervigilance and extreme fear of making mistakes, poor personal boundaries, poor social skills, defensiveness, and hypersensitivity, etc.

Overcoming all this negativity means moving to a place of greater, deeper, and passionate love for ourselves. To expand in your consciousness and move to a place of feeling the love that lies within you, you'll need to:

- Define your worth. Cultivating self-love means living on your own terms, and not anybody else's. Your self-worth is a function of how you value yourself. You must first discover your values if you want to build your self-worth and make up your own definition of success. As such, you must define your integrity, establish what you believe and the kind of person you want to be, as well as how you want to live your life. However, you must ensure to keep all of these within the context of what is realistically attainable. By creating your own values, you get to rely on yourself rather than depend on others to decide what's best for you. It's your life, so, own it.

- Pay more attention to your thoughts and filter your perceptions. To combat negative thoughts, you must become more aware of your thoughts. Awareness helps us to disengage from negativity. Focus more on positivity. You have to totally accept yourself and understand that you are a perfectly imperfect human being, as are we all. Complete acceptance comes from knowing that we cannot always be perfect. We all make mistakes, don't let your past keep you down longer than necessary. Allow yourself to fully express your perfection and don't let negativity hold you back. Let go of self-judgment and any projected judgment of others you had chosen to believe. Do not be limited by them. Instead, allow yourself to be what you truly are. Embody love in everything that you do by cultivating self-love.

- Create a new environment. Avoid environments or situations that reinforce feelings of negativity or low self-worth. Instead, be more in environments where you feel confident, accepted, happy, and prosperous.

Always seek to play to your strengths and concentrate on your natural aptitudes instead of struggling against something that will cause you to feel less successful. Shun critical and judgmental people and form associations with supportive friends who are always willing to shower you with love and make you happy.

- Work on yourself. Change the things about yourself that you feel you can. Don't like your dress style? Change it. How about your hairstyle and makeup? Do you feel confident in them? If yes, then don't let anyone tell you otherwise. Change what you can and accept what you can't.
- Set boundaries. It's your life, you have the right to create firm boundaries that others must not cross. Decide for yourself how you want to be treated and what you won't tolerate. This way, you won't let people have their way with you. People love and respect individuals with principles. Communicate boundaries and act assertively when necessary.
- Simplify and create balance. Having a complicated, overly scheduled life can be exhausting. Aim to create a balance by cutting back on unnecessary tasks, duties,

and commitments that do not add to your life. By doing this, you create space, so you can better work on yourself, pursue your passion, and redefine how you want to spend your time and energy.

- Deal with past wounds and practice forgiveness. If there is something from your past that keeps reminding you of how unworthy you are of the life you aim to live, deal with it. Talk to a counselor who can help you overcome past pain and teach you new ways of relating to yourself and others. Also, you must forgive others who hurt you if you want to move ahead and cut ties with past pains. It is also crucial to forgive yourself for past mistakes. Holding onto grudges won't undo the harm done you in the past. Your ability to forgive and let bygones be bygones can help you to attain wholeness much faster and easier than you thought. Compassion is the hallmark of great women.

Learning to love yourself is a process. The more you practice the strategies outlined above, the easier they become. And as you do, you will begin to feel a general sense of peace that you have never experienced before. With every mindful effort your make, you will discover that you respect and see yourself as deserving of your own love.

CHAPTER THREE

How to Practice Self-Care

In an ever-busy world, finding the time to take proper care of ourselves can be hard. Sometimes, we focus so much on our goals, achievements, and meeting the high expectations we have of ourselves to take care of ourselves. However, engaging in self-care activities enables us to cope with stress and improve our overall well-being. To successfully practice self-care, you need to understand your own needs including emotional, physical, and professional desires. Understanding your needs and putting yourself first occasionally will enable you to better take care of yourself and your responsibilities.

You can practice self-care in the following ways:

Emotionally:

- Manage stress. Emotionally, one of the better ways to take care of yourself is to make conscientious efforts to reduce stress. Do not take up more responsibility than you can handle at one go. Practice relaxation techniques like deep breathing, yoga, etc. to help increase your energy and motivation.
- Make time for fun. Don't be too busy working that you forget about fun and leisure. Engaging in fun activities will help you to reduce stress. Fun things you could do include watching a movie, having a date night, listening to music, etc.
- Surround yourself with supportive friends. Spend quality time with supportive people and those who make you feel good about yourself. At this point in your life, what you need are people who will encourage you to go for your goals and not individuals who will drain, belittle, or stress you out.
- Encourage yourself. Eliminate negativity in your thoughts. Always seek to encourage and validate yourself by saying positive things such as "I can do

this," "I am my own heroine," "I love and accept myself with all my flaws," etc.

Physically

Physically, you can take care of yourself by doing the following:

- Eat healthy/Drink lots of water. Committing to a healthy diet can be one of the smartest decisions you will ever make. Nutritious foods improve health and keep you energized. Eating the wrong foods can leave you feeling unhealthy. Foods you can incorporate into your diet include whole grains, lean proteins, low-fat/fat-free dairy products, fruits, and dark green vegetables.
- Do not forget to exercise. Exercise plays a vital role in building and maintaining muscles and bones. Physical activity also offers mental benefits such as stress relief. Make it a duty to stay active. Try wearing a pedometer and/or having fun activity challenges with friends. Exercises you could do include taking your dog for a walk, running, doing yard work, yoga, or even dancing in the house. Find what works for you and have fun!

- Sleep. Adequate sleep is a vital aspect of a healthy lifestyle. Sleep for between 6 to 9 hours each day. Adequate sleep helps to boost memory, spur creativity, curb inflammation, and sharpen your focus, among other things.
- Monitor your physical health. Make it a point to see the doctor at least once each year. When sick, take some time off work and take prescriptions and vitamins religiously.

Professionally:

- Make your workplace comfortable. Being in a workplace that makes you feel calm, competent, and motivated helps to reduce stress and improve your productivity. You can create a comfortable workspace by decluttering your desk, getting a cozy and comfortable chair, wearing noise-canceling headphones to allow you to work without distraction, etc.
- Schedule regular breaks. While at work, take frequent breaks. Walk around between intervals to clear your

thoughts when stressed. Rest when you feel tired. Get something to eat when you feel hungry.

Mindful Ways of Shifting into a Positive Mindset

Life is full of ups and downs. Experiences can make it hard for us to stay positive and happy. In our everyday living, we face disappointments, hurt, worries, rejections, illnesses, annoyance, jealousy, etc., which can make it easy for us to fall prey to negative thinking. Negative thoughts drain us of energy and prevent us from living in the present. The more we surrender to negative thinking, the more it takes control of us. Once we start having negative thoughts, it becomes hard for us to stop them or shift our focus into a positive mindset.

However, shifting our focus to positive thoughts is crucial if we must avoid living a life of pain and misery. Some of the things we can do to overcome negative thoughts and shift into a positive mindset include:

- Meditation/Reiki. Meditation helps our transition from a negative thought to a positive thought. Meditation works because to meditate, we need to have a clear mind and not think about anything else but focus on our breathing. When we meditate, our mind and brain set to a blank state. Meditating for say, 10 minutes enables us to clear our head and feel relaxed and ready to focus on positive thoughts.

- Surround yourself with positive people. The company you keep has a huge impact on your thoughts. Happiness, they say, is contagious – so is negativity. To stay positive and happy, it is critical that you surround yourself with positive people, not the kind who are negative and jealous of everything you do. When you allow yourself to be lifted by the positive vibes of others, you can easily face each day with spirit. Be with people who know how to nurture and create their own happiness.
- Develop your mental strength. Your ability to maintain focus on the positive despite the difficulty faced can mean the difference between having a positive and negative mindset. Look to improve your tolerance, patience, and concentration, and see how much more of a positive person you'd be. Building mental toughness will allow you to keep your thoughts

and self-talk positive and avoid habits that lead to negativity and unhealthy behaviors. With a tough mental strength, you won't waste precious time feeling sad and sorry for yourself. Instead, you will learn to accept the situation as it comes and seek ways out of it. You can develop mental toughness by choosing to stay positive no matter what, focusing only on the things you can control, keeping your emotions in check, and preparing your mind to accept that bad moments come around occasionally.

- Remember that perfection is elusive. We all desire to live a certain way, look a certain way, but we never quite reach or attain what is in our imagination because perfection doesn't exist. Perfection and flawlessness are impossible to reach. So, before you dwell on your mistakes, you would do well to remind yourself nobody is perfect. It is worth reiterating that we have all made mistakes in the past. And none of our mistakes matter when we show a willingness to become a better version of ourselves. The only thing you could do is learn from your mistakes and move ahead with your life.

- Read motivational quotes. Motivational quotes cheer us all up. Reading inspirational quotes helps to boost our motivation and enable us to act towards what we want. In addition, reading inspiring quotes leads to a happier and more fulfilling life. It makes you realize that others have been in your shoes before, giving you hope that you too can overcome. Every bad moment is a passing phase, reading motivational quotes reminds us of that.
- Live in the moment. Too much focus on the future or past often leads to negative thinking or stress. Do not waste time replaying past moments or worrying too much about the future that you fail to take advantage of the moment that is right before you. The present moment is the only moment you have control over right now, so you must make it count.
- Find a reason to be thankful. Gratitude is not my natural disposition, so this took some time and effort. It was a discipline to remind myself of the many reasons I have to be grateful. But it was an exercise well worth the discomfort. How about being thankful for health and for the fact that you are still alive? The

world is full of pain and suffering, disappointment and regret, hardship and turmoil. Be thankful for the little things in life.

Here's my challenge to you: Take some time today, wherever you are and whatever you're doing, to come up with a gratitude list. If it doesn't come naturally, don't let that stop you from still giving thanks.

Deciding to see the positive side of things is a choice that you must make if you want to become whole. With efforts and commitment, you will learn to focus your thoughts entirely on the positive aspects of things and shun the negative.

grateful
thankful
blessed

CHAPTER FOUR

Define Your Purpose

The importance of articulating the purpose in your life cannot be overemphasized. One of the most important discoveries any person can make in life is finding their life's mission, the reason for their existence. As humans, nothing gives us inner wholeness and peace like a clear understanding of where we are headed.

If you want to get ahead in life, it is essential that you learn to define your end goal. Defining your purpose gives you a clearer picture of where you are going. Articulating your mission and planning your life is key to success. Purpose guides your life and enables you to apply the appropriate processes and actions to achieve your goals. According to Clayton Christensen in the book "How Will You Measure Your Life?" there are three processes that take you through the steps you need to define your purpose. They include:

- Likeness. This concerns what want your life to become when you are at the end of a road. In this manner, a likeness is what we hope to make of our life or career at the end of it all. Discovering what you want to do, whether in your career, lifestyle, or anything else, is crucial to defining your purpose, as it will help you to pinpoint what you want from your future or out of life.
- Commitment. Without commitment, you may find yourself drifting from your purpose much sooner than you expect. By refusing to commit to your mission, you are not giving yourself the chance to succeed. You need to be fully committed to your purpose for it to be useful.
- Metrics. There is little point in setting a goal if you will never know whether you were successful or not. Metrics enable you to measure your progress and see how far you have come. Tracking and evaluating your progress is important in goal setting, as it allows you to determine the level of success you have achieved. When you measure your progress, you can see how you are coming along. The essence of knowing your

progress is that, if you are making good progress, your confidence grows along with your motivation, giving you the drive you need to see your goal through.

A strong sense of purpose fuels your motivation. If you want to achieve success, you must have a definite sense of direction and a clear understanding of what success means to you. The importance of defining your purpose is that it allows you to align your activities with your goals. So, what is your life's purpose? What goal will you be most happy to accomplish? Think about these questions carefully as you go about defining your purpose in life.

> **Bloom**
>
> YOU ARE A GREAT, MIGHTY AND POWERFUL SPIRITUAL BEING WITH DIGNITY, DIRECTION AND PURPOSE.
> ~ROSA BERIGUETE
> EMPOWERMENT & SPIRITUAL COACH

CHAPTER FIVE

Vision Boards

Also known as dream boards, vision boards are visualization tools that refer to any board used to build a collage of words and pictures that represent our goals and aspirations. This way, a vision board helps us to clarify, concentrate, and maintain focus on a specific life goal. Creating a vision board will enable you to get clarity on what is most important to you, remain focused on what matters the most, and point your life in the direction you choose. Vision boards are inspirational collages that serve as your image of your future, that is, a tangible example, idea, or representation of where you are headed. In this manner, vision boards represent your dreams, goals, and what you consider an ideal life.

Images, they say, speak louder than words.

Representing your objectives with images allows you to strengthen and stimulate your emotions because the human mind responds strongly to visual stimulation. Once you develop an emotional attachment to your goals, you will find you become more committed to achieving them. After defining your objective, illustrate them visually using a vision board and see how much impact it will make.

You can obtain a vision board in either of two ways: buy it from a professional supplier or make one using cork or poster boards. Making visual representations of your purpose in one space allows you to quickly visualize them and get all the inspiration you need without having to flip the pages of a diary tucked far away. Make it a duty to look at your vision board at least once every day. With time, you will develop an attachment to your goals.

How to Use a Vision Board for Goal-Setting

Vision boards help you to relentlessly pursue your dreams and achieve your goals by continually reminding you about the goals you set out to accomplish. As a result, you will discover you always seek ways to realize your goals.

For maximum efficiency, put a vision board in a place where you can see it every day. Doing this will inspire you to visualize your ideal life on a constant basis. Vision boards work because visualization stimulates the creative powers of our subconscious mind and programs our brain to note resources that were always there but escaped our notice.

We attract into our lives whatever we are focusing on (the law of attraction). Through the Law of Attraction, visualization also magnetizes and draws us to the people, resources, as well as opportunities that we need to achieve our goal.

You will naturally become more motivated to achieve your purpose just by making visualization practice a part of your daily routine. You will begin to see that you are usually doing things that move you closer to the life you have always wanted.

With time, you will discover that you are working to become a better version of yourself, asking more directly for what you want, taking on more responsibility, more willing to lead, and more disposed to take risks in your personal and professional life.

How to Create Inspiring Vision Boards

Whether you're trying to lose weight, get a promotion, or create more time for yourself, a vision board is a great way to get started and stay motivated. I rely so heavily on my day-to-day planner that I sometimes lose track of my long-term goals, which can lead me to feel discouraged. So, get inspired and **GET STARTED**! You can make an Empowering Vision/Dream Board in the following ways:

- The first step to creating a vision board that inspires you is to establish what your goals are. You should decide what you want and be very clear about them.
- Gather a bunch of old magazines with gorgeous pictures. Beautiful, attractive photos are inspiring. You can also go online and just print the ones you want.
- Look for pictures that represent your goals and motivate you. Find time and go through the magazines you collected. Cut out images that portray your goals and inspire you in some meaningful way. Go for images that immediately inspire hope the moment you set eyes on them. How an image makes you feel at first sight is very important when it comes to designing vision boards.
- Make a collage out of the pictures collected. Now that you have all the images you need, it's about time you make a vision board out of them. Get a large piece of construction or poster paper from your local craft or dollar store. You can also use a corkboard. On your poster paper, glue, tack, or tape your images in an arrangement that you consider appealing.

- Add inspirational affirmation words that show how you want to feel. Words have power. The basic structure of human thought is language. The language we choose to use each day and the words we choose to speak and think affect our feelings. By adding inspirational affirmative words to your vision board, you become more aware of your daily thoughts and words, which goes a long way in reducing the risk of allowing negativity to slip in. Telling yourself "I am, I can, I received, I am open" are some of the ways you can approach each day, as affirmation affects your subconscious mind and energy level. You could also try to add words like Joyful," "Strong," "Deserving", "Expect", "Victorious", or just any word(s) that capture how you want to feel. Remember to add them to your board in a way that is visually appealing to you.
- After designing your vision board, place it somewhere you can see it every day even without trying to. Seeing your vision board daily will enable you to prompt your subconscious. I like to review my vision board first thing in the morning when I wake up. Also, I review it every night before I go to sleep. I keep my vision board

next to my computer desk where I can see it as often as possible.

> Sometimes we may forget who we are. But what matters most is how quickly we remember our magnificence.
>
> WOMEN EMPOWERMENT CONSULTING, LLC

CHAPTER SIX

Rituals for Self-Empowerment

Self-empowerment is about looking at who you are and becoming more aware of yourself as a unique individual. Self-empowerment involves developing the confidence and strength to *Unleash Your Inner Goddess*. Everyone has strengths and weaknesses and a range of skills that are used in everyday situations, but all too often people remain unaware of, or undervalue, their true abilities.

We experience different types of energies from various sources in our daily living, some healthy, others unhealthy. To remove and wash away unwanted, negative energy, you need to embark on rituals that will help you tap into your own extraordinary self-powers. Some of the routines you can do to empower yourself include:

- Exercise: Exercise of any type is empowering. It strengthens the body and raises dopamine (the main reason why you feel good while exercising). Dopamine helps to stabilize our mental and emotional states. If you want to feel empowered, move, dance, go swimming. Just don't stay in one place. A sedentary lifestyle isn't for you.
- Stop comparing yourself to others: We are unique in our purpose. You do not possess the same talent, quality or attributes as others. As such, always aim to play to your strengths. Comparing yourself to others is unhealthy.
- Affirmations: Speak the right words that make you feel lifted. Always refer to yourself as a winner. Say to yourself, "I can do it if I put my mind to it," and then go on to do it. Speaking positive words will help to strengthen you in your daily endeavors.
- Visualization: A quick meditation goes a long way. You can do yoga or go to a quiet place, close your eyes, and take a deep breath. Daydream as much as you can about the things that you aim to achieve; it can help spur you to greatness. Always seek to picture the

perfect outcome for any problem, desire, purpose, and envisage the life you wish to accomplish. Envisioning how you want your future to look gives you strength and hope that you could still secure a better life.

- Find inspiration: What drives you? What inspires you to become a better version of yourself? What do you want to achieve in your career? If your motivation comes from an activity, then you should find time to do more of that activity. Having a constant source of inspiration allows you to dream bigger and work toward achieving more significant goals in life.

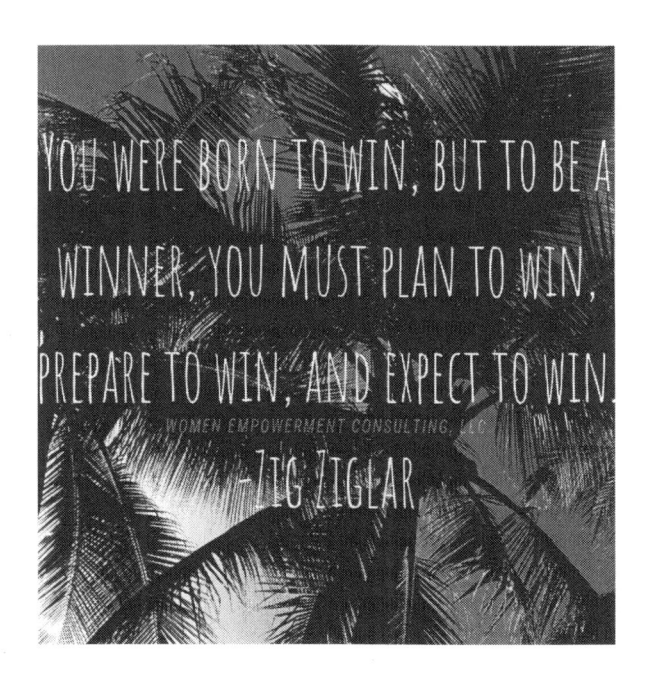

> YOU WERE BORN TO WIN, BUT TO BE A WINNER, YOU MUST PLAN TO WIN, PREPARE TO WIN, AND EXPECT TO WIN.
> —JIG ZIGLAR

Conclusion

Self-love is crucial to self-empowerment. Believing you deserve better than you are currently getting is essential to pushing you toward self-actualization. Caring for yourself, accepting yourself, and not settling for less should form the foundation of your becoming. You need to learn to love yourself when you make mistakes just as much as you love yourself when you are successful. Love the person you see in the mirror with all her flaws. Love yourself when you face setbacks and must try again. Stop existing and start living your life on purpose.

Further, unlearn deeply ingrained beliefs that you are inferior to any other person, or that you cannot make it in life. Replace thoughts of inadequacy and inferiority with positive beliefs. Loving yourself isn't just about loving the person you are. It is also about taking care of yourself physically, mentally, spiritually, emotionally, and professionally, and being kind to yourself despite what you perceive as limitations. Despite all the challenges you have faced in life, you can be your own cheerleader and create the life you deserve. At the end of the day give yourself credit for all that you do. You can be that extraordinary woman you have always wanted to be. From this point forward, *EMBRACE THE GLORIOUS MESS THAT YOU ARE & UNLEASH YOUR INNER GODDESS!!*

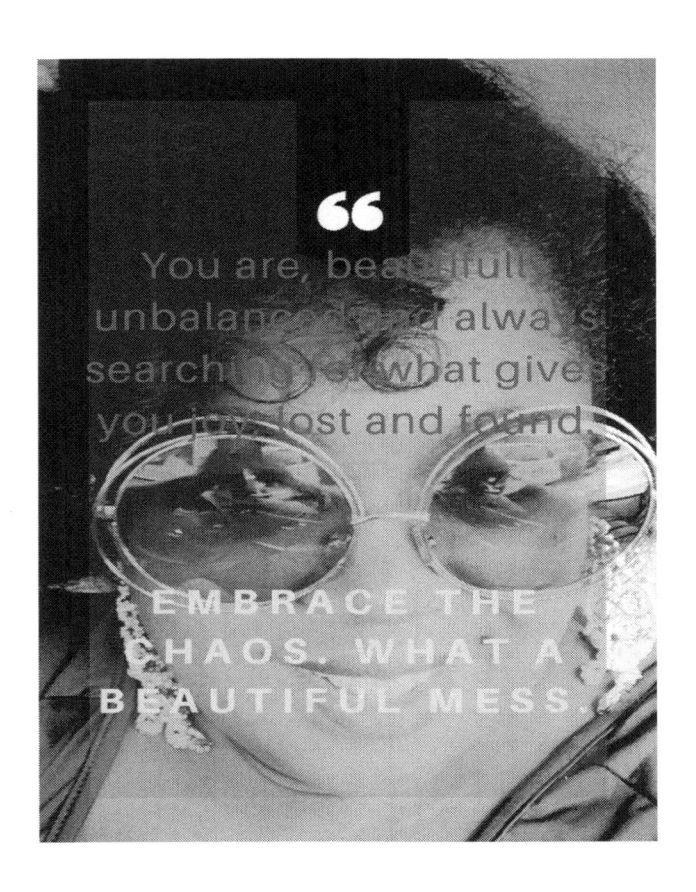

Made in the USA
Middletown, DE
06 March 2019